CONTENTS

H O L O C A U S T

DISCARDED

Voices and Visions

A COLLECTION OF PRIMARY SOURCES

Compiled by:
Dr. William L. Shulman
President, Association of Holocaust Organizations
Director, Holocaust Resource Center & Archives, New York

Series Advisor:
Dr. Michael Berenbaum
President & CEO of Survivors of the
Shoah Visual History Foundation, Los Angeles

Series Editor:
Lisa Clyde Nielsen

*"We were just sitting there talking, and the only thing that we were
saying to each other was, if we ever get out alive, there were two things
that we would like to do. One is to be able to have enough food to eat—
and we thought that would never happen again. And number two, to be
able to tell others of what happened. Although we were sure at the
time—and we said to each other—that nobody's going to believe us."*
—Lee Potasinski, memory from Dachau

A   B L A C K B I R C H   P R E S S   B O O K
W O O D B R I D G E ,   C O N N E C T I C U T

Acknowledgments

Many people have given generously of their time and knowledge during the development of this series. We would like to thank the following people in particular: Genya Markon, and the staff at the United States Holocaust Memorial Museum Photo Archives—Leslie Swift, Sharon Muller, Alex Rossino, and Teresa Pollin—for their talented guidance; and Dr. Michael Berenbaum, currently President and CEO of the Survivors of the Shoah Visual History Foundation and formerly Director of the Research Institute at the U.S. Holocaust Memorial Museum, for his valuable editorial input and his enthusiastic support of our efforts.

Dr. William L. Shulman, President of the Association of Holocaust Organizations and Director of the Holocaust Resource Center & Archives at Queensborough Community College, merits special mention. As the series academic editor—as well as the compiler of Books 7 and 8—Dr. Shulman's guidance, insight, and dedication went far beyond the call of duty. His deep and thorough knowledge of the subject gave us all the critical perspective we needed to make this series a reality.

Published by Blackbirch Press, Inc.
260 Amity Road
Woodbridge, CT 06525

web site: http://www.blackbirch.com
e-mail: staff@blackbirch.com

©1998 Blackbirch Press, Inc.
First Edition

Printed in the United States of America

10 9 8 7 6 5 4 3 2 1

Cover: (clockwise from top left) Thea Sonnenmark; Lee Potasinski; Jane Keibel; Joachim Kalter; Hanne Liebmann; Willi Pohl and his wife.

Library of Congress Cataloging-in-Publication Data

Voices and Visions : a collection of primary sources / compiled by William L. Shulman. —
    1st ed.
        p.   cm. — (Holocaust)
    Includes bibliographical references and index.
    Summary: A compilation of personal narratives of people who survived the Holocaust.
    ISBN 1-56711-207-2 (library binding: alk. paper)
    1. Holocaust, Jewish (1939–1945)—Personal narratives—Juvenile literature. [1. Holocaust,
Jewish (1939–1945)—Personal narratives. 2. World War, 1939–1945—Jews.] I. Shulman,
William L. II. Series: Holocaust (Woodbridge, Conn.)
D804.34.V65   1998
940.53'18—dc21
                                                                            97-2578
                                                                              CIP
                                                                               AC

Introduction

The Holocaust was a period of time from 1933 to 1945 in which approximately 6 million Jews and perhaps nearly 4 million other people were murdered by Nazis and collaborators under Adolf Hitler's regime. Hundreds of thousands, if not millions, of ordinary people across much of Europe helped the Nazis to bring this massive genocide about.

This genocide, however, did not appear out of nowhere; murderous persecution of Jews and other groups had surfaced at various times in Europe for many centuries. Nor did it occur simply because of Hitler's rabid antisemitism (hatred of Jews). It was the result of a number of factors, some of which will be illuminated in the pages that follow.

This volume is both a source book for Books 1 through 6 of the Blackbirch Holocaust series and a collection of documents and eyewitness testimonies that, by itself, tells the story of the Holocaust—the twentieth-century attempt to destroy the Jews of Europe. Most of the first-person testimonies that follow were collected through interviews conducted specifically for this book and have never before been published. They are the memories of ordinary people who survived the extraordinary horrors of those years. It is essential to preserve survivors' stories, because they are the last eyewitnesses to what happened.

The documentation begins with some of the earliest Nazi verbal attacks on the Jews, at a point in time when the Nazis were a small fringe political party. Each document or piece of testimony illustrates a significant event in this history.

Literally millions of documents exist regarding the Holocaust. Because the documents and first-person histories in this volume have been selected to supplement Books 1 through 6 in the series, it is important to read this material as a companion to those books. Each document, each oral history, can thus lead the reader to a greater understanding of the events of that period.

The Rise of Nazism

(to August 1935)

When I was about 10 years old, there was a knock on my apartment-house door, and there was my best friend, Hans. And he spat in my face, and he said, "Manfred, you dirty . . . Jew." My best friend, overnight.

—Fred Margulies

Adolf Hitler (saluting center) presides over a massive Nazi rally in Nuremberg, Germany, September 1934.

"Purifying" Germany of Jews

From its earliest days, antisemitism (hatred of Jews) was a major part of the philosophy of the National Socialist German Workers' (Nazi) Party. In fact, one of its goals was to make Germany "free" or "purified" of Jews—*Judenrein*, the Nazis called it. This aim was clear from the Nazi Party's first statement of goals, presented in Munich, Germany in 1920. According to Point 4 of the program:

> *Only Nationals [Volksgenossen] can be Citizens of the State. Only persons of German blood can be Nationals, regardless of religious affiliation. No Jew can therefore be a German National.*

Point 5 continued the process of separating German Jews from the country in which they had lived for hundreds of years:

> *Any person who is not a Citizen will be able to live in Germany only as a guest and must be subject to legislation for Aliens.*

A Philosophy of Hate

Adolf Hitler wrote *Mein Kampf* ("My Struggle") in prison in 1924. In it, he developed the idea of Jews as the enemy of "Aryans," the people of Northern European stock whom he considered the "true Germans":

> *I believe that I am acting in accordance with the will of the Almighty Creator: by defending myself against the Jew, I am fighting for the work of the Lord. . . .*
> *A racially pure people which is conscious of its blood can never be enslaved by the Jew. . . .*
> *Culturally, he [the Jew] contaminates art, literature, the theater, makes a mockery of natural feeling, overthrows all concepts of beauty and sublimity, of the noble and the good. . . .*

Hitler continued his attacks in his *Zweites Buch* ("Secret Book"), published in 1928:

> *Jewry . . . has special intrinsic characteristics which separate it from all other peoples living on the globe. Jewry is not a religious community. . . . [It] is in reality the . . . governmental system of the Jewish people. . . .*

In that work, Hitler claimed that the Jews sought to weaken and take over Germany and the world and that the Nazi Party alone was fighting against the Jews to preserve humankind.

Anti-Jewish Boycott

A shop labeled for the April 1 boycott.

Among the first actions that Hitler and the Nazi Party took upon coming to power in Germany in 1933 was to organize a boycott, set for April 1, of Jewish businesses and professionals. The instructions for the "Anti-Jewish Boycott" given by the party read:

> *. . . Committees are to be formed immediately for the practical systematic implementation of a boycott of Jewish shops, Jewish goods, Jewish doctors and Jewish lawyers. . . .*

The boycott was reported in the world press. Headlines in the *New York Times* noted: "MEASURE IS EFFECTIVE. JEWS' SHOPS, PLACARDED WITH QUARANTINE SIGNS, CLOSED EVERYWHERE." The boycott was protested throughout the world, but the Nazis were not stopped. They soon moved on to eliminating the Jews from Germany's cultural life. On April 9, 1933, *New York Times* headlines blared: "NAZIS TO CONTROL ALL CULTURAL LIFE. JEWS WILL BE WHOLLY BARRED FROM EXECUTIVE POSITIONS IN THEATRE AND OPERA."

Hanne Liebmann Remembers the Boycott

Hanne Hirsch Liebmann, born in 1924 in Karlsruhe, Germany, described what it was like for German Jews in the early Nazi period:

My father died in February of 1925 and my mother maintained our business, a photo studio. Some of my early childhood memories were of turbulence in the street, and I remember very clearly the first of April 1933. . . the boycott, which meant that all our showcases, our windows, were plastered with decals—"Don't buy from the Jew"—and a brown-shirt [SA; Nazi stormtrooper] standing in front of the window trying to keep people out of our business. And I do believe we didn't do much business that particular day, because surely our Gentile [non-Jewish] customers wouldn't dare to come in, and our Jewish customers stayed at home. . . .

"And I do believe we didn't do much business that particular day . . ."

Forced Sterilizations

It was not only the Jews whom the Nazis wished to eliminate from Germany. In July 1933, their "Law for the Prevention of Progeny with Hereditary Diseases" stated that all people who suffered from diseases that the Nazis considered hereditary—such as mental illness, retardation, physical deformity, epilepsy, blindness, deafness, and severe alcoholism—should be sterilized. It "explained" the "need" for such a law to keep certain people from having children:

[I]t is not only the decline in population which is a cause for serious concern but equally the increasingly evident genetic composition of our people. . . . [C]ountless numbers of inferiors and those suffering from hereditary conditions are reproducing unrestrainedly while their sick and asocial offspring burden the community.

The forced sterilizations began in January 1934, and an estimated 300,000 to 400,000 operations were carried out. Most of the people were patients in mental hospitals and other institutions.

Targeting the Romani

Deported Romani women and children wait at an assembly point in Berlin.

Like the Jews, Romani (commonly but incorrectly called Gypsies) were considered by the Nazis to be social outcasts. Under the Weimar Republic—the German government from 1918 to 1933—anti-Romani laws became widespread. These laws required them to register with officials, prohibited them from traveling freely, even sent them to forced-labor camps. When the Nazis came to power, those laws remained in effect—and were expanded. Many Romani were sterilized against their will under the July 1933 sterilization law.

In November 1933, the "Law Against Dangerous Habitual Criminals" was passed. The police then began arresting Romani along with others whom the Nazis considered "asocial"—beggars, vagrants, homeless alcoholics—and putting them in concentration (labor) camps.

Moves Against Jehovah's Witnesses

The Nazis also began to suppress certain Christian minorities who they felt were subversive to their goals, particularly Jehovah's Witnesses. On July 27, 1933, the Gestapo—the Nazi secret police—closed the printing operation of the Watchtower Society, an organization of the Witnesses. The Gestapo ordered all state-police precincts to search regional Witness groups and organizations with these words: "Confiscation of all materials hostile to the State. Report about results."

Willi Pohl: A Witness Remembers

Willi Pohl, a Jehovah's Witness in Germany, was expelled from his school for refusing to give the Hitler salute. Later, he recalled the experience:

At school the main problem was the Hitler salute, which was introduced as a compulsory greeting in April, 1933. . . . A so-called flag-salute was held on Monday mornings. Pupils and teaching staff gathered together on the sports field, which belonged to the school. The flag was hoisted, and at the top of their voices they sang the German national anthem, and also the Horst-Wessel song or Hitler song. . . . As a Jehovah's Witness, I didn't join in, neither saluting the flag with a Hitler salute, nor singing the national anthem. . . . Several months passed, but after a long summer vacation I was informed that I had to leave the school. . . .

Fred Margulies Recalls Childhood in 1933

Fred Margulies explained the changes for Jews in Germany around 1933:

There was a big change in my father's life and consequently in the life of my family. My father and an uncle of mine who owned the business suddenly found that the business was no longer theirs, it was taken over. The reason that that was done was only because they were Jewish.

I well remember . . . that we lived in an apartment house, and we had to move. The reason we had to move is because we were Jewish. And that, of course, had an enormous impact on me as a child, because . . . I was maybe seven years old—it was my first indoctrination [to the fact] that I was not like any other German boy playing in the street, although my real name is Manfred. . . . My father then had a problem in making a living, and so I was very aware of how different things were.

I remember, as well, being just a kid, that there were boxes being put out on the street corners in prominent places near where we

"All the benches were painted green. . . . Stenciled on the back was *Juden Verboten*: 'Jews Prohibited.'"

lived. And on a poster inside these boxes, behind a sheet of glass, were the editions of Der Stürmer. Being a kid, being curious, not being fully aware of the dangers involved, I used to stand and read and look at this. I very quickly became aware of the fact that I'm looking at, as young as I was, an antisemitic hate sheet. Der Stürmer, as you probably know, was a German newspaper published by Julius Streicher, notoriously antisemitic.

I do remember, and I remember it very clearly, that not too many people stopped and looked at that. It was not that people were crowding around looking at this newspaper. But I remember being there and asking, of course, my father and mother, and being told about not looking at it, not standing there, it was dangerous to your life. Which I found hard to understand, because my best friend at the time was a kid who was not Jewish. His name was Hans. . . . And I found it difficult to accept this change in my life. . . .

Life went on relatively normal, but more signs went up rather rapidly. First it was Juden

> **"Life went on relatively normal, but more signs went up rather rapidly. First was *Juden Unerwunscht*: 'Jews Are Not Desired.' Then, *Juden Verboten*: 'Jews Prohibited.'"**

Unerwunscht: *"Jews Are Not Desired."* Then, Juden Verboten: *"Jews Prohibited."*

I remember distinctly the park in which we used to play, Hans and I. I was probably about eight, maybe seven. All the benches were painted green, as they always are, park benches. Stenciled on the back was Juden Verboten: *"Jews Prohibited."* There were two benches set off in the corner in the park in which we played. They were painted yellow. And stenciled in red on the back of these benches was: *"Only for Jews."*

I remember my friend Hans and I played a dare. He would sit in the yellow benches—he wasn't Jewish. I would sit in the green benches—and I was Jewish. And we used to laugh and giggle about this.

That friend, incidentally, turned into a Nazi, my best friend Hans. When I was about 10 years old, there was a knock on my apartment-house door, and there was Hans. And he spat in my face, and he said: *"Manfred, you dirty . . . Jew."* My best friend, overnight. No more sitting on the park benches as kids from then on.

Smoke to Flame

(September 1935–December 1938)

*And we were running, running just to get away from
there. But some SS men . . . followed us. And we were
trying to hide in a building. . . . They got hold of my
boyfriend. . . . The last time I heard from him was
from Dachau [a concentration camp].*

—Thea Sonnenmark

The Nuremberg Laws

The Nuremberg Laws, passed by the Reichstag (the German Parliament) in the fall of 1935, were the legal framework for the removal of the Jews from German society. Although this process had begun as soon as the Nazis had come to power in 1933, these laws used the concept of "race" as the basis for German citizenship.

According to these laws, Jews were a different "race" from "true Germans." (The Nazis incorrectly categorized "Jewishness" as a "race"; Judaism is a religion, not a race.) According to the Reich Citizenship Law, passed in September 1935:

> *A Reich citizen is only that subject of German or kindred blood who proves by his conduct that he is willing and suited loyally to serve the German people and the Reich. . . .*

In September, the Reichstag also passed the "Law for the Protection of German Blood and German Honor" to limit the place of Jews in German society. One of its provisions stated:

> *Marriages between Jews and subjects of German or kindred blood are forbidden. Marriages nevertheless concluded are invalid. . . .*

The "First Decree to the Reich Citizenship Law" was passed in November 1935. It stated: "A Jew cannot be a Reich citizen. He is not entitled to the right to vote on political matters; he cannot hold public office."

The decree went on to define who was a Jew and the different degrees of "Jewishness":

> *A Jew is anyone descended from at least three grandparents who are fully Jewish as regards race. . . . Also deemed a Jew is a Jewish* Mischling *[a word meaning "mongrel" or "hybrid"] subject who is descended from two fully Jewish grandparents and*
>   a. *who belonged to the Jewish religious community when the law was issued or has subsequently been admitted to it;*

b. *who was married to a Jew when the law was issued or has subsequently married one;*

c. *who is the offspring of a marriage concluded by a Jew, within the meaning of . . . the Law for the Protection of German Blood and German Honor.*

The "First Decree for Implementation of the Law for the Protection of German Blood and German Honor" was also passed in November. It read:

Subjects who are Jewish Mischlinge *with two fully Jewish grandparents may conclude marriages with subjects of German or kindred blood, or with subjects who are Jewish* Mischlinge *having only one fully Jewish grandparent, only by permission of the Reich Minister of the Interior and the Deputy of the Führer, or of an agency designated by them.*

In making the decision, special attention is to be paid to the physical, psychological, and character attributes of the applicant, the duration of his family's residence in Germany, his own or his father's service in the World War, and other aspects of his family history. . . .

The World Watches...and Does Nothing

The world was aware of what was happening in Germany. In a series of articles in September 1935, The *New York Times* described the effects of the Nuremberg Laws. The headlines tell the story: "JEWISH PAPERS BANNED. REICH TO ISOLATE ALL JEWISH PUPILS. RACE, NOT RELIGION, BASIS."

In an article published on September 11, a *Times* reporter quoted the chilling words of Julius Streicher, publisher of *Der Stürmer*, the prominent pro-Nazi newspaper. Speaking before 1,300 representatives of Nazi parties from various countries, Streicher said:

uniforms ready even—so they knew in advance that Hitler was going to attack. . . .

We tried very hard to get exit visas, but it was virtually impossible unless you had a country that was willing to take you in. My uncle—my mother had a brother in London, and he got for us an invitation from his doctor to visit. And on the strength of this invitation we did get permission from the British Consulate, and also because we did have an affidavit to come to the United States, eventually we got permission to enter England. It did not say for how long. And so we packed up our things like

"My father was exposed to a number of indignities. He had to scrub the sidewalk in front of the store with a toothbrush."

everybody else . . . we packed up household goods and my piano. My piano—the only reason my mother took it along, she either felt that maybe we could sell it in England and use the money, because I certainly was not much of a pianist. And also she used it to hide some dollars in the piano so that we would have some money to live on again.

These dollars actually were exchanged for us from Austrian money by a Catholic friend, an old lady who was very very observant in Catholicism, never left her house, never socialized with anybody except to go to church. But after Hitler came, she offered—she offered!—for us to hide valuables in her house and she offered to go to the bank and exchange money for us. This was really an unusual step, and I'm mentioning it because there were Gentiles who were helpful.

German troops march into Austria, 1938.

Jewish Refugees Shunned

From July 5 to July 16, 1938, representatives from 32 countries met at Evian, France, to discuss refugee policies. With the exception of the Dominican Republic, all refused to allow Jewish refugees to enter in numbers above the quotas they already had in place.

Ways to identify the Jews of "Greater Germany" and force them to emigrate and to eliminate them from economic life were set forth by the Nazis in the month following the Evian Conference.

Joachim Kalter: Expelled from the Third Reich

I begin with the day of my expulsion from the German Reich, October 29, 1938. The cause of this was a measure by the Polish government, which had announced that all Polish citizens who had not lived in Poland since 1918 would be deprived of their citizenship. This law was to take effect on November 1. In reaction, the German government decided to expel all Polish Jews from its territory as quickly as possible. My own experience thus resulted from the hostility of both the Polish and German governments.

On this fateful morning, I was picked up by the Gestapo together with my family, and taken to the police station nearest our home. The measures were draconic, but did not overstep the bounds of civility due to us as foreigners. We were magnanimously allowed one small suitcase per person, on the grounds that "it is only for two days." We had no reason to mistrust this claim, and followed the "well-meant" advice of the police.

From the police station, where hundreds of our fellow sufferers had already gathered, we were taken by car to the main train station, one of the largest in Europe. There, we were immediately loaded into railroad cars (type 1870) which had been held ready for us. Of course, we were locked in, so that—God forbid—none of the valuable cargo should escape. The Reich Representation of German Jews also arrived, having received permission to give us food and other necessities. One hour later, we left the home we had come to love, travelling to an unknown destination. At every large station we passed, Jewish residents provided us with food, so that at least we did not lack in this respect.

We arrived in Beuthen, on the Polish border, near midnight. The hall of the train station was already overfilled with thousands of our fellow sufferers from all parts of the Reich. The Gestapo guarded the exits; now for the first time I saw these sadists drop their carefully cultivated mask and mercilessly use their rubber truncheons against anyone—especially women, whose complaints were the loudest. As a result of these beatings, nearly half of those in the station hall had to be evacuated and (as we later discovered in Poland) transported back to their homes.

> "I saw these sadists drop their carefully cultivated mask and mercilessly use their rubber truncheons against anyone— especially women, whose complaints were the loudest."

Unfortunately, we belonged to the half who remained in the hall, and waited another six hours before reaching the customs inspection. Even this was possible only with the help of a German sanitation official, who revived my mother after she had fainted. The customs officials treated us courteously, and the inspection was superficial. Money, however, was taken from my father and transferred to my uncle in Leipzig, who was a German citizen. We were astonished to learn later that my uncle had actually received this money. Such thoroughness impressed us; my father especially still believed in German honesty and love of order. At that time, we had not yet been convinced of the opposite.

Kristallnacht: The November Pogroms

On November 9, 1938, the German government ordered the first major pogrom (mob violence) directed against Jews to take place under its control. During the course of the night of November 9–10, violence exploded against Jews throughout Greater Germany. People's homes and businesses were broken into

A synagogue destroyed in Germany during *Kristallnacht*.

and looted. More than 1,000 synagogues were damaged or destroyed. Thousands of Jewish men were arrested and sent to labor camps.

This infamous night, the November Pogroms would become known as *Kristallnacht*— "Crystal Night," or "Night of Broken Glass."

It was a turning point, an indication of just how far the Nazis were willing to go to eliminate the Jews.

Thea Sonnenmark: *Kristallnacht* in Vienna

During *Kristallnacht,* Thea Sonnenmark was in Vienna, Austria. Years later, she explained what that night was like:

On November ninth, a friend of mine, a boyfriend and I, were in the inner city of Vienna, walking. Actually, I had all this time very little trouble walking in Vienna or going any-where because I was blond and blue-eyed and they thought I was a typically Aryan-looking girl.

And so he and I were walking there when we all of a sudden heard a lot of noise around us, unusually much. And it was like crashing or something breaking. And we also saw flames where there shouldn't have been any. We didn't know what happened. And we actually tried to get away from there. But as we ran out of the city we saw flames in other areas, and we realized when we passed them that these were synagogues being burned. By that time, it was going into evening already, and it was dark, and you could see the flames better. And you also heard the noise, of course.

And we were running, running, running just to get away from there. But some SS man or the police, I don't remember exactly, followed us. And we were trying to hide in a building. And we stayed inside the building waiting for them to leave, but they never did. So

"And we also saw flames where there shouldn't have been any."

we came out. They chased after us. They let me go, they got hold of my boyfriend. They took him with them. The last time I heard from him was from Dachau, and he was killed after that time, in Dachau.

Little Action

The events of *Kristallnacht* were reported around the world. But, even in the face of this violence, Western governments did little to help the Jews—although they now had an inkling of what might be the consequences. In fact, many Jews fleeing Greater Germany were refused entry to other countries.

This policy was summed up in a telegram sent by the American ambassador to Great Britain, Joseph Kennedy (father of the future president of the United States, John F. Kennedy), to the U.S. secretary of state, Cordell Hull, on November 14, 1938.

> . . . *With regard to the countries of refuge, that is, the countries surrounding Germany, I shall report that the illegal crossing of frontiers by refugees had [reached] such proportions that the local authorities of these countries can no longer cope effectively with the situation. The consequence is that they have been obliged to ship refugees back to Germany indiscriminately and with a disregard of the probable consequences to the unfortunate people, many of whom have been immediately thrust into prison camps.*

Emboldened by the Western powers' reluctance to confront them, the Nazis now moved to achieve Hitler's "final aim": the elimination of European Jewry.

The Blaze Engulfs

(January 1939–December 1941)

And from the ship we appealed to Mr. Roosevelt. . . .
They did not want to let us in. . . . We saw Miami and
New York, and nothing happened, so we sailed to
Europe.

—Jane Keibel

The *Kindertransport*: Leaving for Shelter

By 1939, many Jews were trying desperately to leave Germany and Austria. One such effort was the *Kindertransport*, or "Children's Transport"—convoys of children from Germany and German-occupied territories who were able to leave the European continent for temporary or permanent shelter. Ellen Alexander was one of those children.

Ellen Alexander: Sent on the *Kindertransport*

At the age of nine—maybe before then—I became very much aware of what was going on in the world, in Berlin, actually, because we were not allowed to play with the Aryan children. And people would call their children away from us because we were Jews and therefore not clean, not fit to be played with. We had to leave our school. We had to go to Jewish schools.

The school that I went to with my older sister was in Berlin. I don't know exactly which school it was, but it was attached to a synagogue. And the day that—on November 10, 1938 [Kristallnacht], we came to the school, and it was in flames. And I do remember seeing people standing around and laughing and having a wonderful time watching these flames. And that I think was probably the end of our schooling. I didn't understand the import of

all this, but it certainly made an impression on me.

How my parents got us to go on the Kindertransport I don't know, but on May 3, 1939, my sister and I were sent to England. And my parents were not overly emotional, although they may have been, especially my mother, but she didn't show it. And we were able to leave with a lot of other children to go to an unknown place, a place where we didn't know the language. But that didn't bother me much. I was young, and everything was an adventure.

After we left—after the children, my sister and I left—my father was not able to work for himself or for his father-in-law anymore and was eventually made to sweep the streets under some young little Nazi boy who he had to help. He had to carry the bricks and he had to sweep the streets and do very very menial work.

My sister and I were in England and had a pretty happy life, all in all. I couldn't complain about our foster parents. But our parents were sent to Theresienstadt [a concentration camp in Czechoslovakia] in 1943, and I never saw my father again.

Refused Entry

Another effort to get out of Germany was made by German Jews who were able to secure passage to Cuba on the S.S. *St. Louis.* On May 13, 1939, a total of 937 Jews departed Hamburg on this luxury liner. All had visas—permits that assured them the right to land. But when they arrived, Cuba refused them entry. When they then attempted to reach the shores of the United States, the ship was forced out of U.S. territorial waters by the Coast Guard, on orders of the U.S. government. Jane Keibel was a child on that voyage.

Jane Keibel Remembers the S.S. *St. Louis* Voyage

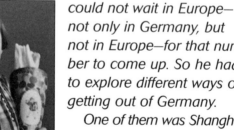

My father had a business, like a five-and-dime store. And he kept the store open until Kristallnacht. And then he had to close the store and he had to hand it over to the Nazis. . . .

We had our visas to America for quite a while, because my father had two brothers who lived here. But my immigration number was very high. And after Kristallnacht, *my* father decided he could not wait in Europe— not only in Germany, but not in Europe—for that number to come up. So he had to explore different ways of getting out of Germany.

One of them was Shanghai, China, and he was not looking forward to that, so he opted for Cuba. And he bought visas for my family, my sister, myself, and my parents. And if I remember correctly, they were $1,500 apiece.

And after he got the visas, the entry visas to Cuba, he purchased places on the ship. And the ship that had room was the St. Louis. *And that left on May 13, 1939. . . . My father spent all his money on this, we went first class. And my sister and I shared our cabin with a distant relative, a lady who was supposed to chaperone us.*

We boarded the ship on May 13, 1939. It was a German ship and it sailed out of Hamburg in the afternoon. It took about 10 days to reach Havana. And when we got to Havana, we weren't supposed to land at the port, but we had to stay out in international waters. And the excuse was that the Cuban authorities had to come and inspect passports and visas.

And they came on board, and they inspected, and they left, and we still couldn't land. We were told after a couple of days that the reason we couldn't land was the Cuban government wanted more money. And the passengers on the ship, of course, had no money—all we were allowed to take out of Germany was 10 dollars.

"So Jewish organizations…tried to raise money…. But whatever money they raised was not enough for Cuba…. They did not want to let us in."

So Jewish organizations got involved and tried to raise money, mostly out of America. But whatever money they raised was not enough for Cuba.

And from the ship we appealed to Mr. Roosevelt, who was the American president then, and the children sent a telegram to Mrs. Roosevelt, but nothing became available. They did not want to let us in.

The orders were from the shipping company to come back to Europe, to Germany. So we went up the coast, we saw Miami, and we went up as far as New York, and nothing happened, so we sailed to Europe. . . . Just before we reached the English Channel, four countries said they would take a quarter of the passengers. And we went to France.

On June 6, 1939, the *St. Louis* returned to Europe. Only last-minute decisions by Great Britain, Holland, France, and Belgium prevented the refugees from returning to certain incarceration in Nazi concentration camps. Still, many of those who remained on the continent ended up in the camps.

Germany Attacks Poland

Hitler declares war on Poland, 1939.

Germany attacked Poland on September 1, 1939. Numbering about 3.3 million people, Jews made up about 10 percent of the population of the country. There were many towns and cities throughout Poland with large Jewish settlements. In their hundreds of years in Poland, the Jews had established a culturally rich and socially and politically complex society—as had other Jewish communities in Eastern Europe that would also be eliminated.

Lee Potasinski Recalls the Invasion of Poland

Lee Potasinski had grown up in Bendzin, Poland. After the German invasion, his family fled to the town of Jenju, hoping to outrun the German advance. At the time, he was about seven years old. Later, he recalled:

We had no idea how the Germans would behave. Consequently, everybody was very innocent. One thing we did do was nobody walked down the street.

And after the fourth day, the Germans decided to call all Jewish males into the market. And among them was my uncle. The Germans claimed, as they had all the males rounded up, that two

German soldiers had been killed, which later on we found out was not true. And they took all the males who were assembled at that time, and they were all shot, right then. That was, so to speak, the eye-opener and the beginning of what we saw would be the end of everything.

My father then, of course, my father was not assembled. My father hid out. Two days later, he decided to go back to Bendzin, where we lived all these years, and when we came to Bendzin, all Jewish homes, all synagogues, were either burned down or were all on fire. Germans used to take Jewish people and bring them into the synagogue, take all the prayer books, and all the Torahs out, put them in the street, pour gasoline, and put a match to them.

Little by little the Germans started applying pressure. They used to make announcements that Jews are not allowed to walk on certain streets; that Jews, if they do walk on certain streets, are not allowed to walk on the sidewalk. If a Jew sees a German officer on the sidewalk, even if he

". . . when we came to Bendzin, all Jewish homes, all synagogues, were either burned down or were all on fire."

is allowed to walk on that street on the sidewalk, he has to step off the sidewalk and walk in the gutter.

And this type of harassment, whether it was the street or whether they'd come in the house, continued; I mean it was 24 hours a day. They used to knock on your door at night and come in, they'd either look around or they'd take the males with them and sometimes children with them and that was the end.

"Overall Measures": Elimination of European Jewry

Forcing Jews to live in ghettos and stripping them of their freedom and dignity in other ways were stages in a process of ultimate destruction.

On September 21, 1939, before the fall of Warsaw, Poland, Reinhard Heydrich, a high-ranking SS officer, sent an express letter to the leaders of the *Einsatzgruppen* (mobile killing squads). It dealt with Jews in the German-occupied territories and said in part:

[T]he planned "overall measures" (i.e. the final aim) [the elimination of the Jews] are to be kept "strictly secret." Distinction must be made between:

(1) The final aim (which will require an extended period of time), and

(2) The stages leading to the fulfillment of this final aim (which will be carried out in short terms).

The planned measures demand the most thorough preparation in their technical as well as economic aspects. . . .

For the time being, the first prerequisite for the final aim is the concentration of the Jews from the countryside into the larger cities. This is to be carried out with all speed. . . . The aim should be to establish only a few cities of concentration . . . it is to be borne in mind that only cities which are rail junctions, or at least are located along rail lines, are to be designated as concentration points. . . .

In each Jewish community, a Council of Jewish Elders [Judenrat] is to be set up. . . . The council is to be made "fully responsible" for the exact and punctual execution of all directives issued or yet to be issued. . . . The reason to be given for the concentration of the Jews into the cities is that Jews have most [sic] participated in the guerrilla attacks and plundering actions. . . .

For general reasons of security, the concentration of Jews in the cities will probably necessitate orders altogether barring Jews from certain sections of cities, or, for example, forbidding them to leave the ghetto or go out after a designated evening hour, etc. However, economic necessities are always to be considered in this connection. . . .

It is clear that a great deal of preparation for these actions against the Jews had to have taken place long before Germany's invasion of Poland.

The *Judenrate*

Members of the *Judenrat* in the Cracow ghetto, 1940.

The Jewish Councils (*Judenrate*) of which Heydrich spoke were in a very difficult position. The people who made up these Councils were part of the Jewish community—but they were also required to fulfill the Nazis' directives.

The strategy of most of them was based on two assumptions: that Nazi Germany would ultimately be defeated, and that not all the inmates of the ghetto would survive. But they were in a desperate situation; often they had no choice but to bend to the will of the Nazis. Wrote historian Raul Hilberg:

The traditional role of the Jewish community machinery—to educate the children in the schools, to feed the hungry in soup kitchens, and to help the sick in its hospitals—was now supplemented by another, quite different function: the transmission of German directives and orders to the Jewish population, the use of Jewish police to enforce German will, the deliverance of Jewish property, Jewish labor, and Jewish lives to the German enemy.

The Jewish councils continued until the end to make desperate attempts to alleviate the suffering and to stop the mass dying in the ghettos. But at the same time, the councils responded to German demands with automatic compliance and invoked German authority to compel the community's obedience. Thus, the Jewish leadership both saved and destroyed its people.

"Mercy Death"

It was not only the Jews who underwent severe persecution in 1939. In October of that year, Hitler approved a decree giving doctors the power to "grant a mercy death" (termed euthanasia) to "patients considered incurable according to the best available human judgement of their state of health." The intent of this program was to exterminate the mentally ill and the handicapped, thereby "cleansing" the "Aryan race" of people considered genetically defective and thus a "burden" to society.

In October 1939, the Reich Ministry of the Interior sent a letter to institutions and nursing homes. It asked that all patients be reported who

1. suffer from the following diseases. . . : schizophrenia, epilepsy, senile diseases, paralysis, insanity, encephalitis, Huntington or other neurological fatal fits or

2. have been for at least five years permanently in institutions or

3. are kept as criminally insane or

4. do not possess German citizenship or are not of German or ethnically related blood.

"Resettlement"

A father and son await deportation in Cracow, 1941.

In October 1939, orders were issued to begin the deportation (shipping) of Jews from Austria to camps in German-occupied Poland. The Nazis called this "resettlement." A Nazi directive detailing the deportation of Jews from Austria to Nisko in October 1939 ordered:

[T]he Resettlement operation to Poland will begin at 22.00 [8:00 P.M.] on October 30, 1939, with the first transport of 1,000 Jews fit for work, from the Aspang Rail Station in Vienna. . . .

Further transports will leave regularly on Tuesdays and Fridays of each week with 1,000 Jews. The second and third transports will consist of Jews and Jewesses at present under arrest in Vienna, whose departure date has been set by the Gestapo. From the fourth transport on, complete families will already be sent.

. . . In addition, each transport is accompanied by 25 police officers under the command of a police captain, who must prevent all danger of escape by use of arms.

Similar arrangements were made for Jews from other areas of Greater Germany.

Official documents prove that the United States government was aware of developments throughout this period. On October 20, 1941, a telegram from Berlin to the U.S. secretary of state in Washington, D.C., stated: ". . . [It] is anticipated that under present plans all Jews in Germany will be deported within a few months."

The Ghettos

In Poland, Jews were concentrated in ghettos, or "Jewish quarters," of the larger towns and cities. The first was established in Piotrkow; the second in the industrial center of Lodz.

Ghettos were set apart from the rest of the community. They generally were surrounded by a wall and were located in the poorest areas. The non-Jewish population was ordered to move out in order to make room for the Jews from outlying villages and other areas of the city or town.

Propaganda

Part of the Nazi propaganda effort was to persuade non-Jews that the ghettos were necessary to "protect" them from the Jews, who the Nazis said were carriers of epidemic illnesses. Jews were also accused of cooperating with Germany's enemies. But the real reason behind the establishment of the ghettos was to remove the Jews. And, as far as epidemics were concerned, the overcrowding of the ghettos created them, and the number of Jewish victims was tremendous.

A telegram that was sent on October 14, 1941, from Berlin to the U.S. secretary of state in Washington, D.C., addressed the German propaganda:

The revival of the Jewish question by the required wearing of the Star of David [a Jewish symbol] has met with almost universal disapproval by the people of Berlin and in some cases with astonishing manifestations of sympathy with the Jews in public. This reaction has become increasingly obvious to all observers. To combat it, the newspapers periodically publish attacks on the Jews, accuse them of violating the rationing restrictions and assert that Berliners are dissatisfied at the continued existence of such parasites in their midst. The party organization has now begun distributing leaflets to households urging people to avoid all contact with Jews and to shun the Star of David with disdain when they encounter it on the street.

Isolation

Residents of the Lodz ghetto are directed at a crossing between two areas of the ghetto.

The ghettos established by the Nazis differed in many ways, including the degree of isolation from the outside world. In Lodz, Poland, there was literally no possibility of contact with the world outside. The ghetto was fenced in with barbed wire, and exits were guarded by police who had standing orders to kill. Food was strictly rationed.

In certain other ghettos, smuggling and economic exchange eased the hardships of isolation. But even there, poverty was such that the starved population could not buy even the meager supplies that were available.

Emanuel Ringelblum: "It Came Like a Thunderbolt"

In November 1940, the ghetto in Warsaw was established. It soon became occupied-Poland's largest forced concentration of Jews. The chief chronicler of the Warsaw ghetto was Emanuel Ringelblum. He wrote:

The Saturday the Ghetto was introduced was terrible. People in the street didn't know it was to be a closed ghetto, so it came like a thunderbolt. Details of German, Polish and Jewish guards stood at every street corner searching passersby to decide whether or not they had the right to pass.

"Catastrophic"

A destitute woman sits with four children in the Warsaw ghetto.

Even Nazi officials recognized the hideous conditions in the ghettos. In an official monthly report for April 16 through May 15, 1941, a German military officer described the Warsaw ghetto:

The situation in the Jewish quarter is catastrophic. Dead bodies of those who collapsed from lack of strength are lying in the streets. Mortality, 80% undernourishment, has tripled since February. The only thing allotted to the Jews is 1½ pounds [.68 kilograms] of bread a week. Potatoes . . . have not been delivered. . . . The ghetto is growing into a . . . breeder of illness and the worst subhumanity. . . .

The Situation in France

Western Europe was not immune from the Nazi menace. Thousands of German Jews were sent to Gurs, a concentration camp in German-occupied France. As was noted by "Matthews" in this telegram from Paris to the U.S. secretary of state in Washington, D.C., the French were unprepared for their arrival:

The camp commander was upset as he had had but three hours notice prior to their arrival. . . .

The local press here has, of course, been told to make no reference to this. The fact that in the face of existing severe rationing and food shortages France is to be burdened with the care and feeding of at least 4,000 additional foreign "refugees" (and they may be the forerunner of other arrivals) will hardly tend to diminish the unpopularity of the government's new found Nazi "friends."

Hanne Liebmann Remembers: Deportation to France

On October 22, 1940, early in the morning, the police arrived at our house to arrest us. And we didn't know why we were being arrested, and it turned out, to be deported. Our household consisted of six women: my paternal grandmother, my mother and I, and three of my mother's sisters. . . .

So here were 12 police and Gestapo people arresting six women from the age of 91 ½ down to 16. We were given an hour's time to pack, one suitcase or about 50 kilos [110 pounds], as long as we could carry it. We were told to take a blanket if possible; a fork, a spoon, a knife; and some provisions for about two or three days. This represented a problem, because at that time there was food rationing in Germany, and Jewish people received smaller rations than the general population. Also, one didn't keep three days' food in the house, so we were already left with a deficit. . . .

We were taken by an open police truck to the railroad station. Now, my almost-92-year-old grandmother, of course, had extreme problems getting up on the truck. She was a lady who always wore long skirts, a long coat, high boots, and she simply was stuck in the fashions of 1910. . . . It presented a problem because the risers on the side of the truck were no bigger than maybe half your foot, so she could not really get a hold on it, and it was extremely difficult to get her up. There were people standing in the street watching this thing, how I struggled with her, to get her up on the truck. And they really thought it was very funny and had great smiles on their faces. . . .

There were already quite a number of people at the railroad station by the time we came. We were assembled there, all 950 Jews from the city of Karlsruhe. . . .

By evening, we were put on trains. These were old third-class passenger trains with wooden benches. We were allowed to take very little money. And if you had the money in your house, fine, otherwise you were out of luck.

We were on the train from the 22nd of October till the 25th of October. Conditions on the train were horrendous. Never would we have imagined that later on people would be transported in cattle cars.

The situation was terrible, simply because we had such an overage population, very few young people, middle-aged people. We received food, as far as I can remember, once, when the train stopped in Mulhouse [in France, called Mulhausen in German]. That meant we were going into France. And as it turned out, we were the only group of people ever to be deported to the west, from Germany to France. All other transports went east.

We had no water. Whatever little food people had, we didn't know how long it had to last. And my grandmother, who was basically all right at home, functioned, knew everything—due to hunger and the stress, and whatever, lost her mind. She absolutely lost her mind. She begged to be undressed, to be put to bed, to go to sleep. And it was over and over again, "Take off my shoes . . . give me my slippers . . . I want to go to bed." And of course, we couldn't. . . .

When we arrived at our destination, the train was left standing on the railroad track for many many hours before we were taken off. And it was on the 25th of October; it was raining very, very hard. We were put on open trucks and trucked to the concentration camp called Gurs. It is about 40 kilometers [25 miles] from the Spanish border. We could in good weather

"We could in good weather see the wonderful-looking Pyrenees, but it didn't help us. We couldn't get there."

see the wonderful-looking Pyrenees Mountains, but it didn't help us. It didn't do anything for us. We couldn't get there.

The conditions in the camp when we arrived: First of all, we were soaking wet, because we were, as I mentioned, in open trucks. Men and women were trucked separately; men and women were in separate blocks. The camp was divided by a main road, the only paved road. It had at the beginning of the camp some administrative buildings and a so-called hospital. It did have blocks, numbered from A to M. Each block consisted of about 25 barracks. Each block was surrounded by barbed wire. And then, of course, the whole camp again was surrounded by rows of barbed wire. Also there were ditches around each block. They were about, I would say, three, four feet deep [about one meter].

We were put into wooden barracks, very flimsy wooden barracks. There was absolutely nothing in these barracks. Some had a table and maybe two benches, about five or six feet long [about 2 meters]. A light bulb at each end. A door at each end. And I believe maybe six or eight hatches—we didn't have windows, it was a hatch that opened up. You had to prop it up in order to have it open. Now, if it opened and it rained, water would come in; if you closed it, you were in the dark and you didn't have any fresh air.

The barracks were covered with a single layer of tarpaper, which in many places was torn, and water would come down on us. And you really couldn't move away, because the barracks were filled to capacity. There were no cots, or anything. So we had to sleep on the floor. We were given straw the first night. Not everybody had straw to lie on.

Eventually, we were given some cotton sacks to put the straw in, to make something like a makeshift mattress, but very thin and insufficient. . . . We found my grandmother two weeks later in the camp. She did not know where she had been, what had happened to her. Neither could she appreciate anymore where she was.

They had a barracks for the old, sick people, and they had cots for them. So we left her over there, so she would not have to be lying on the floor. Once down on the floor we would not have been able to get her up anymore.

> **"What was in the soup was mostly old vegetables. But not what you buy here in the supermarket—what you usually feed to animals."**

The food in camp, like in all camps, consisted of about half a pound [one-quarter kilogram] of bread a day, something that resembled coffee in the morning, a watery vegetable soup with occasionally a couple of small pieces of meat. The same in the evening, or sometimes only tea. Occasionally, we would get a small portion of brown sugar. I don't know, or don't remember if we got anything else in addition to the steady diet. . . .

There was a time in Gurs where there was nothing else but pumpkin. Pumpkin every day, morning and evening, for weeks on end. Some people almost turned yellow from that thing.

What was in the soup was mostly old vegetables. But not what you buy here in the supermarket—what you usually feed to animals. And this was basically our diet. . . .

In the beginning we did not know if the world knew that we were deported, where we were, or what. Neither did we know if we could write letters, or receive letters. It turned out that we could, which was a big help, a big support. We were even able to get some money from the outside, *if you had friends or relatives who were able to spare some and send it to you.*

Toilets were latrines, [they] were built up about five or six feet [two meters] off the ground. It did have stalls, individual stalls, but in most cases no doors. It was simply a concrete slab with holes in it and a huge pail underneath. So we all had to first learn how to use these latrines. And of course something like toilet paper or any of this— forget it. Anything we ever knew that was civilized life had now disappeared, in one quick stroke.

We had a lot of people who got ill with dysentery. If young people got sick with it, they very quickly died. There were absolutely no medications available.

Sanitary facilities were extremely poor. We had water three times a day, for two hours, morning, noon, and night—two hours each barracks, which meant you had to really make a beeline to get water to drink, wash yourself, do your laundry, or whatever.

In the beginning we had to wash outdoors, in the open. The women got a washroom eventually; the men never did. They always, no matter what the weather was, no matter how cold or how hot, whatever,

"Anything we ever knew that was civilized life had now disappeared, in one quick stroke."

they had to wash outdoors—by the way, in plain sight of the main road of the camp.

There was no privacy, obviously, whatsoever, at any time.

There was, however, one thing in Gurs and some of the other camps that existed in France. That was that social services from various organizations could function. One of them was the Swiss Red Cross, the Children's Division; a Jewish welfare agency for children; the Catholic and Protestant Church Social Services; and the Quakers. And they were of great help to everyone, especially the Red Cross, who had an additional meal for young people in the morning. Some of the worst cases of malnutrition of the adults were also given some food by the Swiss Red Cross. The Jewish welfare agency was very active in the camp, trying to get children and young people out . . . and they did a magnificent job. They did a magnificent job all during the war helping children survive. At one point a social worker came to my mother and asked her whether she would let me go to a place called Le Chambon because there were a Huguenot [a Protestant group] people and a minister who were interested in getting people out of the camp to help them survive—to go to school, to have a fairly normal life. And my mother asked me, and I said yes. . . .

I myself, together with six other young people from the camp, including a young lady who was with me in the same barracks, left on September 8, 1941, to go to Le Chambon. It was certainly the great adventure of our lives to go to a place we had never heard of, didn't speak the language, knew nothing about. But we left, and, while we were happy to leave, our hearts also broke because we left our parents behind and other relatives.

We came to Le Chambon, and we were received very wonderfully with a good meal, with stuff we hadn't seen in a long long time. And we were placed in a group home. The group home was run by the Swiss Red Cross Children's Division. Everyone in this village was helpful to us, looked out for our best interests, and made our as good life as it could possibly be made under the circumstances.

Most of us went to school. Yes, we were happy to be where we were, but also unhappy that our parents were left in the camp. So it

> "Everyone in this village was helpful to us, looked out for our best interests, and made our life as good as it could possibly be made under the circumstances."

was a two-edged thing. Our parents and our family in the camp were a constant worry to us—in the beginning when we came to Le Chambon, we could not eat all the fat we were given; after 11 months our stomachs were very small. And so we would toast that bread very very hard, make a package, send it to the camp, and hope they could somehow make some sort of porridge out of it or whatever.

We would, frankly speaking, steal some potatoes in the fields, from the farmers, to send them off to camp, because a potato was something very very precious, nobody ever saw a potato in the camp.

So, while we were happy to be where we were, to have decent food and wonderful people around us, people who taught us great lessons, we also had the steady worry about our parents. Life in Le Chambon was as normal as it possibly could be for us, living in a group home, which is not a normal life, essentially. Going to school. It was just a wonderful place to be for us during that time.

When the time came, when the French came to round up Jewish people in August–September 1942, no questions were asked, we were hidden by the farmers, they took almost impossible, and attempts were punished with death. Even if it succeeded, flight from the camp would have been useless. Patrols combed the countryside, and the Poles could not be relied on, for they too risked their lives if they helped fugitives. Moreover, where could one flee? The cities had now been cleared entirely of Jews, except for the newly established ghettos. Even these were swept by monthly pogroms, which progressively reduced the Jewish population to isolated pockets awaiting evacuation. By early 1943, the plan for removing Jews from Poland had largely been fulfilled.

I learned afterwards that my older brother was deported to the crematoria in September 1942, followed by my mother three months later. She had already given me up for dead, and could not bear the loss of two sons; her life became meaningless to her. My father and younger brother remained among the 300 Jews left in the city. Months later, I received a postcard, on which my mother had written several lines before her last journey. It was addressed to my father, who sent it on to me. These lines showed my mother's entire heart and her love for her family. She wrote: "I am going where I can find peace. Don't worry about me. Hold together and think of Achi [Joachim]." Not a word about herself; she always thought of others.

"... my mother ... had already given me up for dead, and could not bear the loss of two sons; her life became meaningless to her."

Felice Ehrman: "A Rude Awakening"

Felice Ehrman was a teenager in 1942. She tells what it was like being sent to Theresienstadt, a concentration camp near Prague, in German-occupied Czechoslovakia.

On March 18 or 19, 1942, we went on a transport to Theresienstadt. We arrived there March 22. I stayed there until the end of the war.

We were lucky. We didn't go on cattle cars; we went on a regular train. It took about three days. We were allowed to take whatever we could carry. That means a knapsack and probably two bags.

My grandparents were really not that old, they weren't as old as I am now. But they were very old—they were old in their thinking, they were old physically. I think that the lack of antibiotics in those days took a great deal out of them every time there was any kind of an illness. My grandmother had pneumonia and it took her three months to recuperate. Today it takes a week or two and that's it. I think that showed. And it was a very stressful situation for them. They really could not adjust to this whole horror.

When we got there, we were put into a barracks meant for the cavalry. We were put in what used to be the stables on the main floor, the ground floor, with only straw on the floor. Then the Germans came, and we had to line up all our luggage. They went through all our luggage. They took away what they called contraband: They took out salt, they took out toothbrushes, they took out combs, all sanitary articles. Somehow they did leave the food. We didn't have that much food with us, because, you know, you didn't know exactly what to take. So, I think we didn't have very much food, and besides, we really couldn't take cooked foods, so we had some baked goods, quickly baked, some bread, and maybe some cheese, but really not that much.

> **"And in the morning, they took us to a large room, and they shaved us. And that was such an unbelievable shock…"**

That was at night. And in the morning, they took us to a large room, and they shaved us. And that was such an unbelievable shock, because all of a sudden I looked at my grandmother, who was standing next to me, and literally did not recognize her, because hair is such an important part of your looks, of the way you look.

My grandfather had magnificent white hair and a goatee and a little mustache, and without the mustache, and without the goatee, and without any hair, he looked almost like a caricature. His ears were sticking out. And he was such a handsome man, and all of a sudden, he was just— I mean, I was crying, I couldn't help myself. It was just such an awful sight. . . .

We were assigned a large room, which had wooden triple-decker– double triple-deckers—in other words, each bed, so to speak, each bunker had room for six people. And we had straw mattresses, they looked almost like potato sacks that they had filled with straw. And we took our knapsacks, and we used our knapsacks for a pillow, and whatever blankets we had. And that's how we got started there. It was quite a rude awakening, to say the least.

Focus on the Young

The Nazis didn't give any special treatment or leniency for Jewish children. In fact, they were especially interested in the elimination of the children. The following SS order, which focuses on the Jews of France, illustrates the urgency with which they wanted to accomplish this goal:

> *Subject: Removing Jews from France*
> *. . . French police will carry out the arrest of stateless Jews in Paris during July 16–18, 1942. It is expected that after the arrests about 4,000 Jew-children will remain behind. . . . Inasmuch . . . as any lengthy togetherness of these Jew-children and non-Jewish children is undesirable, and since the "Union of the Jews in France" is not capable of accommodating in its own children's homes [e.g. orphanages] more than 400 children, I request an urgent decision by letter as to whether the children of the stateless Jews about to be deported may be removed also. . . .*

The "Final Solution" in Poland

The first step in the Nazis' mass murder of the Jews of Europe was to gather them together so that they might be sent to their destruction in an "efficient" manner. Heinrich Himmler, the head of the SS, gave the following orders for completion of this task in German-occupied Poland:

> *I herewith order that the resettlement of the entire Jewish population . . . be carried out and completed by December 31, 1942. . . .*
> *These measures are required with a view to the necessary ethnic division of races and peoples for the New Order in Europe, and also in the interests of the security and cleanliness of the German Reich and its sphere of interest.*

Voices from the Warsaw Ghetto

Children of the Warsaw ghetto

The following excerpts from Warsaw ghetto residents give a picture of the Warsaw ghetto in the summer of 1942—and the anguish of the people living there. Wrote Avraham Levin on June 5:

People die in great numbers of starvation, the typhus epidemic or dysentery, they are tortured and murdered by the Germans in great numbers, but they do not escape from life by their own desire. On the contrary, they are tied to life by all their senses, they want to live at any price and to survive the war. . . .

On July 20, Adam Czerniakow wrote about the deportation of ghetto residents to "resettlement" camps in the East that he would have to help implement as a member of the Jewish Council:

It was announced to us that the Jews, without regard to sex or age, apart from certain exceptions, would be deported to the East. Six thousand souls had to be supplied by 4 o'clock today. And this (at least) is how it will be every day. . . .

The person in charge [of the deportation] called me into the office and informed me that my wife was free at the moment, but if the deportation failed she would be the first to be shot as a hostage.

Sending his people to nearly certain death was too great a burden for Czerniakow. The next day, he committed suicide.

On August 5, 1942, the Nazis deported the children from Janusz Korczak's "Child's Home," an orphanage in the Warsaw ghetto—but to where, they didn't know. The *Judenrat* tried to save Korczak, but not the children. He refused, choosing to stay with the youngsters even to their destruction.

On April 23, the Warsaw ghetto revolt commander, Mordecai Anielewicz, gave encouragement to the resisters. In what proved to be his last letter, he outlined what should be done next:

It is impossible to put into words what we have been thorough. One thing is clear, what happened exceeded our boldest dreams. The Germans ran twice from the ghetto. . . . Our losses in man-power are minimal. . . .

Beginning from today we shall shift over to the partisan tactic. Three battle companies will move out tonight, with two tasks: reconnaissance and obtaining arms. Do remember, short-range weapons are of no use to us. We use such weapons only rarely. What we need urgently: grenades, rifles, machine-guns and explosives. . . .

The Stroop Report

Jürgen Stroop, an SS major general and major general of the Nazi police in the Warsaw district, reported to his superiors on the Nazis' "grand operation" to quell the Warsaw ghetto uprising. The following brief excerpt from the Stroop Report indicates the violence of the Nazis' repression of the Warsaw uprising of April and May:

Of the total 56,065 Jews apprehended, about 7,000 were destroyed directly in the course of the grand operation in the former Jewish quarter. 6,929 Jews were destroyed via transport . . . making the total number of Jews destroyed 13,939. In addition to this figure of 56,065, an estimated 5,000 to 6,000 Jews were destroyed in explosions or fires.

Inferno

(July 1943–April 1945)

*Those who could move, most of us, were given some
kind of liquid which they called soup, nobody
touched it. And I remember the first night, that
was in June, we slept outdoors that night, on a
wooden bench. And I can tell you that I never
slept so soundly since then, as that night.*

—Lee Potasinski

Cover-Ups

As the murder of the Jews increased in intensity, the need to hide the mass killings became a concern of the German government. The Nazis did not want Jews to engage in resistance activities. They also did not want the Allies to take actions of revenge against Germans. Thus, a Nazi directive stated:

Where the Jewish Question is brought up in public, there may be no discussion of a future overall solution. . . . It may, however, be mentioned that the Jews are taken in groups for appropriate labor purposes.

Panic in the Ghettos

As word of the genocide spread among the Jewish population, Jews began to try to escape from the ghettos. A Nazi report stated:

. . . Rumors were spread in the various ghettos that [actions] would take place within a short period in which not only children, old people and the unfit would be shot by the Security Police, but all the inmates of the ghettos without exception. . . . As a result, there was something like panic in the various ghettos, particularly in the Vilna [Vilnius, Lithuania] ghetto. In two peat-cutting camps near Vilna the Jews tried to escape and to join a group of bandits [partisans]. In a third peat camp an atonement measure [murder] was carried out. . . .

Slowly but systematically, the ghettos were liquidated. That is, Jews of all ages were put on trains and sent to death camps. The lucky ones—those who had some particularly useful skill and stamina, or who were in the right transport—were sent to slave-labor camps as an interim step before their murder.

In 1944, the Jews of Hungary—the last major Jewish population group remaining by that time—were rounded up. They were put in ghettos and then deported to camps.

Stephen Berger Remembers the Round-up in Hungary

Stephen Berger explained what happened to him in Hungary in 1944:

After all our possessions were stripped away from us, the next step was the setting up of the ghetto in one part of the city. They designated the streets. They made actual fences, wooden fences with one gate where you could go in and out, with a Hungarian policeman posted at the gate. And within a certain period of time every Jew had to be in the ghetto. . . .

A few friends and I decided to go out from the ghetto and try to get some food in town. Of course the only way you can go out from the ghetto is by illegal means, because the ghetto is sealed. We managed to go out from the ghetto at night, through the fence. We hid during the night outside the ghetto, and next morning, when stores opened in town, we tried to buy some food. And hiding with the food during the day, we tried to get back the following night—smuggled the food back into the ghetto.

We did this quite successfully a number of times, and then one day our luck ran out. We were in a small grocery store, and it so happened that the former neighbor of ours recognized me. And before we knew it,

he went to the police, informed the police about us buying food. And when we came out from the store, the whole neighborhood was surrounded by the police. . . . Among all the policeman, a small army, we were unarmed. Really, we were youngsters. But, of course, they considered us as an enemy of the people. They took us to the police station. They put us under intensive interrogation. And that meant we were beaten. But they couldn't find anything on us except the food we purchased. They took us back into the ghetto. . . .

I think that was the first time really we had an inkling that there was more in store for us than just being there in the ghetto. And sure enough, they liquidated first the small ghetto— we had a big ghetto and a small ghetto—they took the small ghetto and put the small ghetto into the big ghetto. Now we were concentrated only in one spot.

The following day, early in the morning, the Hungarian gendarmes, [policemen] they were even brutal with their own peasants, so you can imagine how much mercy the Jews have gotten—lined us up on the streets of the ghetto ready to march us out to the railroad. And we marched through the streets of

Debrecen, to outside of the town, the old and the sick put on horse-drawn wagons. And also, it was, I recall, fairly early in the morning. We had quite a reviewing from the Hungarian population, lined up on both sides of the street, laughing and clapping their hands, in happiness that they are getting rid of their Jewish citizens.

Now a different phase starts. . . . There is a railroad track, the conditions are deteriorating rapidly. The people are hungry. The sick have no medication. Constant beatings. The wealthy tortured to give up their valuables. They come in with lists. They pick out the wealthy Jews, they take them back to headquarters, torturing them, women or men, to tell where they are hiding their valuables. They come back bloody, with broken bones. . . .

Then one morning, the cattle cars pull in. They are closed cattle cars. And we have our possessions only what we can carry now in a backpack. My mother always tried to look ahead, so she had some dry baked goods or some bread with us. And we are waiting to be loaded up in the cattle cars.

"And we marched through the streets of Debrecen. . . . We had quite a reviewing from the Hungarian population, lined up on both sides of the street, laughing and clapping their hands, in happiness that they are getting rid of their Jewish citizens."

Now, as I remember, there were three trainloads of Jews that went out from our town. Two of them went to Auschwitz directly. One started to go to Auschwitz, turned around, came back to Hungary, and then went to Austria, to Strasshoff, which is a small village outside of Vienna. Strasshoff was a regular concentration camp with barbed wire, towers, barracks, wooden barracks—with the exception that there was no gas coming from the showers.

. . . I was, for some reason, on the train that turned back from Auschwitz and went to Strasshoff.

We were on the train for at least four days, if not more. And about 80 to 86 people in each cattle car, you couldn't sit. We were standing up next to each other, like holding up each other, it was so crowded.

The most horrible thing ever happened to me was that train ride, because there were no sanitary facilities. . . .

And even me, who was in top condition at the age of 16, after four days, I remember very vividly that I was, sort of, my mind was in delirium. I couldn't think straight. I was disoriented. At times I didn't know where I was. These were like flashes, because, after all, I was young and strong. But I can imagine those of the old, and the weak.

Never once during this time we traveled, never once the doors were opened for anything. The smell was unbearable. The cries, the constant cries. The constant moanings.

When we arrived to our point of destination—and we didn't know where it was at the time—they opened those rolling doors, and we just tumbled right out. We had about three or four dead, which I didn't know until they opened the door, because they were just standing up with the live ones.

And they didn't even give us time to recoup. They were waiting right by the railroad yard, these auxiliary Nazis from the Ukraine. . . . They were wearing a different-color uniform, it was a light green uniform instead of the dark green the Germans were wearing so we could distinguish them.

So they were driving us toward the camp, beating everybody over the head with sticks. My mother got a blow on her head. She lost her hearing in one of her ears; even today, she doesn't hear in that ear. We got driven into this concentration camp. And I remember it was early in the afternoon when we arrived. They had driven us into the barracks. We had to undress and take showers. Before that, there was a selection. They took the old and the sick, and they shipped them to Auschwitz. Those who could move, most of us, were given some kind of liquid which they called soup, nobody touched it. And I remember the first night, that was in June, we slept outdoors that night, on a wooden bench. And I can tell you that I never slept so soundly since then, as that night.

Elie Wiesel: *Night*

At the age of 14, Elie Wiesel was taken to Auschwitz–Birkenau. Later, before liberation, he was moved to Buchenwald. Wiesel, who would later win the Nobel Prize, wrote a moving book about his experiences, called *Night*. In the following excerpt, Wiesel captures a sense of the enormous human pain and loss of the Holocaust.

An SS non-commissioned officer came to meet us, a truncheon in his hand. He gave the order: "Men to the left. Women to the right." Eight words spoken quietly, indifferently, without emotion. Eight short, simple words. Yet that was the moment when I parted from my mother. I had not had time to think, but already I felt *the pressure of my father's hand: we were alone. For a part of a second I glimpsed my mother and sisters moving away to the right. Tzipora held mother's hand. I saw them disappear into the distance; my mother was stroking my sister's fair hair, as though to protect her, while I walked with my father and the other men. And I did not know that in that place, at that moment, I was parting from my mother and Tzipora forever. . . .*

By the summer of 1944, most of the Jews had already been murdered. Those who survived to that point could only hope that the Soviet [Allied] armies would reach them before the Germans completed their destruction. Those who weren't killed were forced on death marches to concentration camps in Germany.

- - - - - - - - - - -

Joachim Kalter: "The Push Against Hitler"

Summer came, and with it the invasion, the push against Hitler and the Soviet offensive, which steadily neared our area. We knew that our fate now stood on the razor's edge; at the approach of the Red [Soviet] Army, the Germans would either kill us or, if they had time, evacuate us westward. On July 26, 1944, we could already hear the cannon of the advancing front. That morning the order came: Prepare to march in the afternoon. We were again loaded into closely guarded freight cars, and accompanied by the camp leaders we left this blood-drenched spot. Our journey lasted eight days, more waiting than traveling, for military transports had priority. Finally, we arrived at the Birkenau siding in Auschwitz.

We had already been three days without water, and a great panic now broke out. On the platform beside the train, we heard the voices of our old commandant and the SS receiving officer at Auschwitz. The latter claimed that he had orders from Berlin to send the entire transport to the crematoria. Our camp commandant opposed this energetically, pointing out that we were all experienced inmates, with skills that the Reich needed badly. He received permission to call SS headquarters in Berlin, which answered with an order that we be put to work. We had been saved again for a time.

Our next stop was a well-equipped bathhouse next to the crematorium, where we were de-loused, tattooed and issued zebra-striped inmates' clothing. I received the number A-18160. Then we were put in quarantine, where I met a survivor of my father's transport. I learned from him that my father, after living through three selections, had been sent to the gas chamber because of his age and growing weakness. But my younger brother was still alive in Monowitz-Buna, where he worked as a valet for the SS commandant; he had been sent there after recovering from an attack of typhus. Now that I knew of at least one member of my family who survived, I wanted more than anything to find him and see the end of the war with him. At the moment, I was still in the shadow of the crematorium, where people from among us were sent daily, people who had survived years of concentration camp, and were now killed for some small weakness.

Lee Potasinski: "The Germans Were Hiding"

From Auschwitz, they took us into Germany again. They took us to a camp, Kaufering. Well, the train ride was, I'd say about a week.

This is the middle of 1944. They brought us into Kaufering at night. And I can tell you that the conditions in that camp, the physical conditions, were worse than Auschwitz. There were no barracks. They made holes in the ground and covered it up with wood, and those were, so to speak, sleeping quarters. . . .

We worked under horrible conditions in that camp. We must have walked at least eight to ten miles [13 to 16 kilometers] each way. And I can tell you that every single day, whether it was going to work or coming back to work, we left with a certain amount of people, but we always came back with fewer people. A lot of people were beaten to death on the way to work or they were shot to death.

And in that camp, most of the guards consisted of Ukrainians, and it was unbelievable what they did to us.

We were there about three or four months. And as the Allies were getting closer, they tried to keep us

> "I took my shoes off, I left them there, and I started running in the snow. And that was the only way to get to work alive and not be shot on the way to work."

moving. And it seemed that they ran out of transportation, no trains, because they used always all the trains for their own troops, they started marching us. . . .

They marched us for two weeks. It was, it was really, it was hell. Very little food. And as we were being marched, there were a tremendous amount of planes that used to fly over us that were bombing and strafing. And these were Allied planes, I don't recall whether—yeah, well, American planes. We weren't afraid for some reason or other. The more planes we saw, the more shooting we saw, and the more bombing we saw from the planes, the less afraid we were. The Germans, yes, the Germans were hiding and they were running. As a matter of fact, many people were shot to death by the Germans that did not obey the order—or didn't listen—to hide because of the bombings that were going on by the Allies.

They marched us for two weeks until we came into Dachau.

Anne Frank: "The Ever-Approaching Thunder"

Despite the horrors that the victims of the Holocaust experienced, somehow faith in the human spirit managed to exist. A young girl named Anne Frank expressed her ultimate faith in humanity in her famous diary:

It's really a wonder that I haven't dropped all my ideals, because they seem so absurd and impossible to carry out. Yet I keep them, because in spite of everything, I still believe that people are really good at heart. I simply can't build up my hopes on a foundation consisting of confusion, misery, and death. I see the world gradually being turned into a wilderness. I hear the ever-approaching thunder, which will destroy us, too. I can feel the sufferings of millions and yet, if I look up into the heavens, I think that it will all come right, that this cruelty too will end, and that peace and tranquillity will return again.

In the meantime, I must uphold my ideals, for perhaps the time will come when I shall be able to carry them out.

She never was able to do so. Anne Frank died in Bergen-Belsen camp in March 1945—just weeks before the end of the war. She was 15 years old.

From the Ashes: Liberation and After

I walked outside and looked around. . . . I did not see any guards. . . . I realized what had happened . . . . I did not believe it.

—Lee Potasinski

Liberation at Buchenwald and Dachau

In April 1945, Buchenwald and Dachau camps were liberated by the Allies. Foreign correspondents reported the emotionally wrenching scenes. On April 20, headlines in the *New York Times* read: "DESPAIR BLANKETS BUCHENWALD CAMP. . . . HORROR LINGERS IN HUNGER, THIRST AND DEATH EVEN AFTER LIBERATION FROM SS. . . . MANY OF ATROCITIES COMMITTED BY GERMANS ARE DECLARED TOO HORRIBLE TO REPORT." The article continued:

> *The horror of Buchenwald concentration camp continues even though advancing American troops overran it a week ago on the heels of the fleeing SS guards and technically liberated its 20,000 remaining inmates.*
>
> *These wretched remnants of a prison population that numbered 82,000 in March are free in the sense that their German masters no longer are here to bully and torture them and that those who are not too ill can walk freely about their prison camp or even down to nearby Weimar. But they are prisoners still of misery and hunger, and the weaker ones are still literally starving to death. . . .*
>
> *The strongest of the survivors wandered about with buckets and pitchers in search of water to assuage their burning thirst. The last spiteful gesture of the SS guards before they fled was to wreck the camp's water system and empty the reservoirs. . . .*

Lee Potasinski Remembers Liberation

Lee Potasinski was one of the prisoners at Dachau at the time of liberation:

I came into Dachau in the beginning of, in the winter of 1945. And, especially in my case, I was still very young [age 12½], and there was always the fear that any day, any minute, you'll be picked for a selection. And of course, you had to live with that.

There were rumors and talk that the war is coming to an end. And, of course, none of us believed that—even if the war did come to an end— that anybody was going to get out alive. . . .

I recall when we came to Dachau, we came in the middle of the night, and everybody got a blanket. And we were surprised that we were treated so nice, that everybody gets a blanket in the wintertime. We found out that the reason for giving us a blanket is that we slept outside for at least three or four nights. There was just no room. . . .

A lot of people died in Dachau from starvation, malnutrition. A lot of people tried to escape and were caught, because there was no escape. They were either shot or were left standing outside for a day or two in the wintertime, and they died that way.

They kept us in Dachau until the end of March or so. And one day they told us that everybody is leaving. Now, we didn't know whether the whole camp is leaving or certain groups.

You know, it was very strange, because every time they took us from camp to camp, it was always toward the train station. And this time we started walking, and I noticed that we were already out of town, and I said to myself, there can't be a train station. And sure enough, we walked for, I would say, a good two, two-and-a-half

"We walked for, I would say, a good two, two-and-a-half weeks. A lot of people died on that march."

weeks. A lot of people died on that march. We saw a lot of planes overhead. We didn't know at that time whether they were American planes or British.

Until they brought us to a place, Ferenwald, outside of Munich [Germany]. Again, there were no barracks. There was one big room where everybody was piled into, and one kitchen. . . .

Right across from the camp, Ferenwald, there were a lot of woods. And one day there was a rumor flying around that they are going to take us out of the camp and take us to a different camp. There was another rumor that they were going to take us across into the woods and they were going to shoot everybody, because the war was coming to an end. . . .

That rumor to take us across into the woods and shoot us became stronger and stronger. The following day, in the morning—and that was the end of April, beginning of May 1945—there was a tremendous snowstorm. We didn't know what to think. Some said, "Well, it's very good it snows, maybe they'll be so busy with the snow that they won't take us across."

The same day it started to snow, towards the afternoon, somebody came running into the barracks and told me, "You know, I don't see too many guards outside." And I made nothing out of it, and nobody went out to check, because everybody was afraid to go out to check. And we were just sitting there talking, and the only thing that we were saying to each other was, if we ever get out alive, there were two things that we would like to do. One is to be able to have enough food to eat—and we thought that that would never happen again. And number two, to be able to tell others of what happened. Although we were sure at that time—and we said to each other—that nobody's going to believe us.

At about three, three-thirty that afternoon, I walked outside and looked around. And sure enough, I did not see any guards. But I did see—at that time, I didn't know that these were jeeps of course—

I saw two jeeps coming into the camp, and there were four or five soldiers in each jeep. I didn't know at that point, I couldn't recognize an American from an Englishman, but I saw a different type of uniform, and I saw a different type of face.

And I approached the jeep, and one soldier in that jeep, I asked him, "Do you speak Jewish?" And he said, "No, German. But I am a Jew."

At that point, I realized what had happened. Of course, I did not believe it. I knew that the Germans were gone, but it was impossible to believe. I ran back to the barracks, and I started yelling to everybody. There were a lot of elderly people, and everybody embraced each other, but we still didn't know why. We knew that physically nothing will happen to us, but in a way— we did not know what had happened. . . . And at this point, we didn't know what to do.

Displaced Persons

Although liberation of the camps was a victory, that important triumph also created new problems. One of the major consequences of the liberation was the need to resettle the tens of millions of people who had been displaced by the war and the Nazis' campaign. The task was enormous. Some of these Displaced Persons—DPs—would be uprooted for years to come.

Jewish Displaced Persons arrive in Frankfurt, Germany, on their way to Palestine, 1948.

Some Jewish survivors of the camps went to Palestine, part of which was their ancestral homeland. The *New York Times* reported their arrival on July 17, 1945:

Some refugees were still wearing their striped German concentration camp uniforms, with their serial number tattooed upon their foreheads, when they came ashore here this morning from the British liner Matarda, *which yesterday brought 1,164 Jewish survivors from Europe and former refugees who had been in training in Britain for agricultural settlement under Zionist auspices preparatory to departure for Palestine.*

Pogroms in Poland

Many Polish Jews could not resume their lives in their hometowns, due to pogroms—organized mass attacks against them. Reported the *New York Times* on August 21, 1945:

Dr. Joseph Tenenbaum, president of the World Federation of Polish Jews, asserted yesterday that a new wave of pogroms directed particularly against Jews returning from concentration camps in Germany had broken out in Poland.

The federation has received a report that the latest took place in Cracow, he said, where 2,000 returning Jews were assaulted, 500 of them undergoing siege in the temporary quarters of the Jewish community house there while the Provisional Government's police looked on. He charged that it gave evidence of a systematic endeavor by the reactionary elements in Poland to prevent the return of displaced Jews.

Glossary

Aktion A German word meaning "action" or "plan of action." The term was often used by the SS or Gestapo to mean the planned, mass roundup, deportation, or murder of Jews.

Anschluss The German invasion and annexation of Austria on March 12–13, 1938.

Anti-Semite A person who hates Jews.

Antisemitism Hatred of Jews.

Aryans Originally, a term referring to speakers of any Indo-European language. The Nazis used the term to mean people of Northern European background, or members of what the Nazis termed the German "master race."

Concentration Camps Labor camps set up by the Nazis to house political prisoners or people they considered to be "undesirable." Prisoners were made to work like slaves and many died as a result of starvation, disease, or beatings. *Also called work camps, work centers, and prison camps.*

Crematorium A building in the camps that contained the ovens, where the bodies of victims were burned. The term is sometimes used to refer to an oven itself.

Deportation The shipment of victims to the camps, usually by train in cramped and un-heated cattle cars.

Der Stürmer A virulently antisemitic German newspaper ("The Great Storm") published by Julius Streicher.

Einsatzgruppen "Special Action Groups" or killing squads. Part of the SS, their main purpose was to kill enemies of the Reich, especially Jews and Communists.

Euthanasia In general terms, this practice means killing someone as an act of mercy. Under the Nazi regime, the term was used to justify the T-4 Program, which involved the murder of mentally and physically disabled persons.

Extermination Camps Death camps built by the Nazis in German-occupied Poland for the sole purpose of killing people. The most common method of murder used at these camps was poisonous gas. The victims' bodies were usually burned in ovens in the crematoria. The six extermination camps were Auschwitz-Birkenau, Belzec, Chelmno, Majdanek, Sobibór, and Treblinka. *Also called killing centers.*

Final Solution "The Final Solution to the Jewish Problem" (or Jewish Question), the Nazis' term for their plan to exterminate all the Jews of Europe. The term was first known to have been used at the Wannsee Conference on January 20, 1942.

Führer A German word meaning "leader." It was used to refer to Adolf Hitler, dictator of Germany from 1933 to 1945 and head of the Nazi Party.

Genocide The deliberate and systematic murder of an entire race, class, or group of people.

Gentile A non-Jewish person.

Gestapo The Nazi secret police who were responsible for rounding up, arresting, and deporting victims to ghettos or camps. The Gestapo were part of the SS.

Ghetto In Hitler's Europe, the section of a city where Jews were forced to live apart from other groups, in conditions of extreme crowding and deprivation.

Hitler Youth A Nazi youth organization.

Holocaust A term for the state-sponsored, systematic persecution and annihilation of European Jewry by Nazi Germany and its collaborators between 1933 and 1945. While Jews were the primary victims, with approximately 6 million murdered, many other groups were targeted, including Romani, the mentally and physically disabled, Soviet prisoners of war, political dissidents, Jehovah's Witnesses, and homosexuals. It is believed that perhaps as many as 4 million non-Jews were killed under the Nazi regime.

Jehovah's Witnesses Members of a Christian group who were singled out for persecution in Nazi Germany.

Judenrat "Jewish Council," a group of Jews selected by the Germans to run the ghettos.

Judenrein "Purified of Jews," a German expression for Hitler's plan to rid Germany of all Jews.

Kapos Prisoners in the camps who were selected to guard the other prisoners.

Kindertransport "Children's Transport," an attempt to get Jewish children out of Germany, Austria, and Moravia to safety in England.

Kristallnacht "Night of Broken Glass" or "Night of Crystal." November 9–10, 1938, a night of Nazi-planned terror throughout Germany and Austria, when Jews were savagely attacked and arrested, and their property destroyed. *Most accurately known as the November Pogroms.*

Lebensraum A German term for "living space" to accommodate what the Nazis called the "master race" of Aryan people.

Liberation The freeing of the Nazis' victims from the camps at the end of the war.

Liquidation The removal and murder of residents of the ghettos and the camps.

Mischlinge A derogatory Nazi term meaning "mongrels" or "hybrids" that denoted people having both Christian and Jewish ancestors.

Nazi A term describing a member of the Nazi Party or something associated with the party, such as "Nazi government."

Nazi Party Short for the National Socialist German Workers' Party. Founded in 1919, it became a powerful force under Hitler.

Nuremberg Laws "Reich Citizenship Laws," passed on September 15, 1935. These sweeping laws specified the qualifications for German citizenship and excluded from citizenship persons of Jewish ancestry.

Nuremberg Tribunal or Trials The international court set up to try high-ranking Nazi war criminals in Nuremberg, Germany, after the war.

Partisans Groups of independent fighters who lived in the woods or other remote areas and harassed the German Army or the SS in an effort to disrupt their actions.

Pogroms Organized, mass attacks against a group of people.

Reichstag The German Parliament.

Resettlement A term used by the Nazis to make Jews believe that they were being transported to work camps in Eastern Europe, when in fact they were being taken to extermination camps.

Resistance A general term for actions taken by individuals from various countries, both Jews and Gentiles, against the Nazis. Members of resistance groups worked "underground," in secrecy.

Righteous Gentiles Non-Jews who tried to save Jews from Nazi persecution, often at the risk of their own lives.

Romani Commonly but incorrectly called Gypsies, a people originally from India who were singled out for persecution by the Nazis.

SA From the German term Sturmabteilungen,, meaning "stormtroopers." The SA were Nazi soldiers. *Also called brown-shirts.*

Selection The process by which the Nazis determined which victims at the camps would be spared to work and which ones would be killed immediately.

SS From the German term Schutzstaffel, meaning "special detail." The SS began as Hitler's personal bodyguard and developed into the most powerful and feared organization in the Third Reich. *Also called black-shirts.*

Star of David The six-pointed star that is a symbol of Judaism.

Third Reich Reich means "empire." In German history, the First Reich lasted from 962 until 1806, the second from 1871 to 1918. In the early 1920s, Hitler began using the term "Third Reich" to describe his own empire, which lasted from 1933 until 1945.

Untermenschen A German word meaning "subhumans," used by the Nazis to refer to some groups they considered "undesirable"—Jews, Romani, male homosexuals, political opponents, and the physically and mentally disabled.

About the Survivors

ELLEN ALEXANDER received passage from Germany to England in 1939. She has lived in the United States since emigrating from England in 1947.

STEPHEN BERGER joined the Zionist movement after the war, helped European Jews emigrate to Palestine, and contributed to Israel's war for independence.

FELICE EHRMAN immigrated to the United States in 1947. She married in 1951 and has two daughters and four grandchildren.

JANE KEIBEL and her family were able to emigrate from France to the United States in early 1940. Married in 1950, she has two sons and a grandson.

HANNE LIEBMANN met her future husband in the camp at Gurs in December 1940. They married in Switzerland in 1945. In 1948, she and her family immigrated to the United States.

ALFRED LIPSON immigrated to the United States in 1949. He has devoted much time to writing and editing works on the Holocaust. He and his wife Carol, also an Auschwitz survivor, have two sons and four grandchildren.

FRED MARGULIES arrived in the United States in 1947, the only survivor of his family. He is active in many Jewish organizations and in education regarding the Holocaust and reduction of prejudice.

LEE POTASINSKI has lived in both South America and the United States since leaving Europe in 1946. Active in many Jewish organizations, he and his wife have three children and three grandchildren.

THEA SONNENMARK immigrated to the United States from England in 1940. Married, with two children and three grandchildren, she has a strong Zionist background.

Source Notes

Chapter 1:
Page 8: "Only Nationals..." and "Any person who is not...." In Yitzhak Arad, Yisrael Gutman, and Abraham Margalit, editors. *Documents on the Holocaust.* Jerusalem: Yad Vashem, 1981, p. 15.

Page 8: "I believe that I am...." In Arad, Gutman, and Margalit, p. 22.

Page 9: "Jewry...has special intrinsic...." In Arad, Gutman, and Margalit, p. 26.

Page 9: "Committees are to be formed...." In Arad, Gutman, and Margalit, p. 32.

Page 10: "[It] is not only the decline...." *Legal Gazette,* Berlin, 1933. Approved translation.

Chapter 2:
Pages 15–16: "A Reich citizen...," "Marriages between...," and "A Jew is...." In Arad, Gutman, and Margalit, pp. 77, 78, 80.

Page 16: "Subjects who are...." In Lucy S. Dawidowicz, editor. *A Holocaust Reader.* New York: Behrman House, 1976, pp. 48–49.

Page 18: "...The German people...." In Arad, Gutman, and Margalit, p. 83.

Page 25: "...With regard to...." In John Mendelsohn, editor. *The Holocaust: Selected Documents in Eighteen Volumes.* New York: Garland, 1982, Volume 3, p. 200.

Chapter 3:
Pages 31–32: "...[T]he planned 'overall measures'...." In Arad, Gutman, and Margalit, pp. 173–175.

Page 33: "The traditional role...." Raul Hilberg. *The Destruction of the European Jews.* Chicago: Quadrangle Books, 1961, p. 146.

Pages 33–34: "1. suffer from the following diseases...." In Henry Friedlander. *The Origins of Nazi Genocide: From Euthanasia to the Final Solution.* Chapel Hill, NC: University of North Carolina Press, 1995, p. 76.

Page 34: "[T]he resettlement operation...." In Arad, Gutman, and Margalit, p. 144.

Page 34: "[It] is anticipated...." In Mendelsohn, vol. 8, p. 23.

Page 35: "The revival of the Jewish question...." In Mendelsohn, vol. 8, pp. 18–19.

Page 36: "The Saturday the Ghetto was introduced...." In Jacob Sloan, editor. *Notes from the Warsaw Ghetto: The Journal of Emanuel Ringelblum.* New York: Schocken Books, 1975, p. 86.

Page 37: "The situation in...." In Raul Hilberg. *Documents of Destruction.* Chicago: Quadrangle Books, 1971, p. 40.

Page 37: "The camp commander was upset...." In Mendelsohn, vol. 8, pp. 15–16.

Page 43: "Those of us who received...." In Carol Rittner and Sondra Myers. *Courage to Care.* New York: New York University Press, 1986, p. 102.

Chapter 4:
Page 46: "a) To take all measures...." In Arad, Gutman, and Margalit, pp. 251–256.

Page 52: "Subject: Removing Jews from France...." In Jochem von Lang, editor. *Eichmann Interrogated: Transcripts from the Archives of the Israeli Police.* New York: Vintage Books, 1984, p. 133.

Page 52: "I herewith order...." In Arad, Gutman, and Margalit, p. 275.

Page 53: "People die in great numbers...." Abraham Lewin. *A Cup of Tears: A Diary of the Warsaw Ghetto.* Cambridge, MA: Basil Blackwell, 1989, p. 119.

Page 53: "It was announced...." In Raul Hilberg, Stanislaw Staron, Josef Kermisz, editors. *The Warsaw Diary of Adam Czerniakow.* New York: Stein & Day, 1979, pp. 384-385.

Page 58: "...Mr. Gerhard M. Reigner...." Memo in National Archives, RG 84, Geneva Confidential File 1942.

Page 59: "On September 5...." In Arad, Gutman, and Margalit, p. 284.

Page 59: "Awake and fight!..." In Arad, Gutman, and Margalit, p. 139.

Page 59: "An overall plan for the razing...." In Arad, Gutman, and Margalit, p. 292.

Page 60: "It is impossible...." In Arad, Gutman, and Margalit, p. 292.

Chapter 5:
Page 62: "Where the Jewish Question...." In Arad, Gutman, and Margalit, p. 342.

Page 62: "Rumors were spread...." In Arad, Gutman, and Margalit, pp. 457–458.

Page 65–66: "An SS non-commissioned officer...." Elie Wiesel. *Night.* New York: Avon Books, 1960, p. 39.

Page 68: "It's really a wonder...." Anne Frank. *The Diary of Anne Frank: The Critical Edition.* New York: Doubleday, 1989, p. 694.

Chapter 6:
Page 74: "Before I discuss particulars..." In Telford Taylor. *The Anatomy of the Nuremberg Trials.* New York: Alfred A. Knopf, 1992, p. 168.

Page 74: "The real complaining party...." In Taylor, p. 168.

Page 75: "The Land of Israel...." In Raphael Patai, editor. *Encyclopedia of Zionism and Israel.* New York: McGraw-Hill, 1971, Volume 1, pp. 244–245.

Photo Credits
Pages 6, 11: Bundersarchiv, courtesy of USHMM Photo Archives; pages 9, 30 (above): National Archives; page 12: Willi Pohl, courtesy of Watchtower Bible and Tract Society of New York; pages 17, 24: courtesy of USHMM Photo Archives; page 18: courtesy of Alfred Lipson; pages 20, 24: courtesy of Thea Sonnenmark; page 21: Dokumentationsarchiv des Osterreichischen Widerstandes, courtesy of USHMM Photo Archives; pages 22, 48: courtesy of Joachim Kalter; page 27: courtesy of Ellen Alexander; page 28: courtesy of Jane Keibel; pages 30 (below), 69: courtesy of Lee Potasinski; pages 32, 36 (below), 37: Yad Vashem Photo Archives, courtesy of USHMM Photo Archives; page 34: Archives of Mechanical Documentation, courtesy of USHMM Photo Archives; page 36 (above): Jewish Historical Institute Warsaw, courtesy of USHMM Photo Archives; page 38: Hanne Liebmann; page 52: Central State Archive of Film, Photo, and Phonographic Documents, courtesy of USHMM Photo Archives; page 62: courtesy of Stephen Berger; page 67: courtesy of Anne Frank Stichting; pages 72, 73: National Archives, courtesy of USHMM Photo Archives.

Maps and graphs ©Blackbirch Press, Inc.

Index